all the way
through

# all the way through

poems

## KB BALLENTINE

Sheila-Na-Gig Editions

ISBN: 9781962405096
Library of Congress Control Number: 2024946125

Sheila-Na-Gig Editions
Russell, KY
Hayley Mitchell Haugen, Editor
www.sheilanagigblog.com

At first glance, the reader notices KB Ballentine's marvelous command of natural details, images of nature: "Mimosas' woolly blossoms / brush across the rocks." Reading more carefully, though, we see much more. Her real interest is in the interstices between objects, between people, emotions, even thoughts. These interstices in the porous fabric of our lives are the places where meeting takes place. If we find friends, companions, lovers, this is where we meet them; if we lose something or someone, this is where we lose them as well. Ballentine is the poet of those intimate spaces. In "The Space Between Us," she navigates loss by exploring the moment when summer ends and autumn inevitably begins. From that space she declares: "It's always September now — gannets harping the wind, / promise of winter in its chill." There is a long history in modern poetry of juxtaposed images creating meaning and carrying us to places we hadn't expected were there, but few poets achieve this with such ease and honesty. Because we recognize the images as real, they become part of our lives, just as they have for the poet who wrote them. She does not sentimentalize. Animals are animals; plants are plants; people are people, and the world is constantly bringing them into being and taking them away. *All the Way Through* is posed against these facts of the world, whether it considers Kabul or Arkansas, a kitten that is beyond rescue, or a family member lost too early. These poems do not tell us what to do or believe; they simply allow us to sit with them for a while in the felt interstices they create; they help us to understand.

—George Franklin, author of *Remote Cities*
and *What the Angel Saw, What the Saint Refused*

## Acknowledgments

Thank you to the following publications that first published these poems, sometimes in previous versions.

*3Elements*: "The Space Between Us"
*Auroras & Blossom*: "Peace Lies Curled"
*Blue Mountain Review*: "Waiting for Locusts"
*Blue Nib Poetry*: "What Wind Knows"
*Blue Pepper*: "Fear"
*Compass Rose*: "Light Dissolving"
*Dragonfly Magazine*: "Dance the Crumbling Floor," "Unfiltered After Fifty," "Without Asylum"
*Dwelling Lit Journal*: "The Polish of Rain"
*Fiddles & Scribbles*: "Always Fall Forward"
*Fortnightly Review*: "The Lost Heart"
*Grey Sparrow Journal*: "Through Fog, Through Storm, Stars"
*The Healing Muse*: "After Surgery"
*Humana Obscura*: "Listen for the Roots"
*Impspired*: "Aim at the Wilderness"
*I Thought I Heard a Cardinal Sing*: "Blessing of the Birds"
*Jimson Weed*: "Fill the Ocean With Grief"
*Kelp Journal*: "Between Moments," "The Root of the Wind is Water"
*Lothlorien Poetry Journal*: "Answer the Moon," "Fragments of Grace," "Something Given"
*Louisiana Lit*: "Moments, Rightly Placed," "Spring Tide"
*Monterey Poetry Review*: "All We Are," "Portions," "Unsay the World"
*Odd Magazine*: "Unlock the Door"
*Of Rust and Glass:* "Variations on a Text"
*Pendemics Journal*: "Memory," "No Way Back to What Was"
*Pine, Mountain, Sand, & Gravel*: "When We Get There, I Will Have Nothing to Tell"
*Poetry Quarterly*: "To a Red Bird"
*The Pulse*: "Season of Salt"

*Quill & Parchment*: "Equinox," "Rain, Whispering"
*Raconteur*: "In a Dry Month"
*Rose in the World*: "The Darkness We Carry"
*Salvation South*: "How the Light Gets In," "Living With Ghosts"
*Sheila-Na-Gig online*: "Crowding Out the Light," "Every Scar
    Has an Edge," "Footprints in Ash"
*Sparked Lit*: "Slow, Brief Watch"
*Still: The Journal*: "All the Way Through"
*Tennessee Voices Anthology*: "Color of Blood and Shadow"
*Thimble Lit*: "Becoming a Horizon"
*Valiant Scribe*: "Design Restored"
"Walt's Corner": "Last Hour of the Tide"
*Waxing and Waning*: "What Cannot Be Changed"
*Weekly Avocet*: "At Last the Rains Came," "How Is it, the Light,"
    "Leaving Song"
*White Stag Anthology*: "Catching Moonlight"
*Wild Word*: "Cobwebs, Breathing"
*Women Speak Anthology*: "The Almost Invisible," "Heart, Full of
    Seed," "Leafspear of Light"
*Zingara:* "Grief"

For Bill and Suzanne Brown:
mentors, friends, and, most of all, soulmates

*Ice pellets whistled*
*down my collar*
*feet bare and wet, turning blue*
*but not cold*

*Smiling I reached out*
*but her face darkened and*
*she turned her back*
*and I was cold*

David Austin

*The best way out is always through.*

Robert Frost

# Contents

## I.
*the choir of evening descends*

## II.
*Salt scours my heart, sharp sting of loss*

## III.

*the bargain with light has begun*

## IV.

*night's elegy on their tongues*

## V.
*stardust breathing*

# Muse

—after Beth Paulson

myooz/ verb without object/ 1. To meditate,
to think in silence as a recluse ruminates;
syn: ponder, reflect; in autumn's fading light,
the photographer *muses* about her next composition

/verb with object/ 2. To meditate on, to comment
thoughtfully or ruminate upon; jazz percolates
the room, bartender *musing* how sax and keys
riff the pulsing air, seek the shadows of the night

/noun/ 1. Any of the nine daughters of Zeus
and Mnemosyne concentrating on a particular art;
Clio cradles scrolls of papyrus, *Muse* of history,
keeper of memory

2. Power inspiring a poet, artist, thinker, or the like;
the artist's paintings lay half-finished, abandoned
as the *muse* eluded him for weeks; ant: dismiss, neglect,
forget

# Memory

       is a desperate songbird
hiding in a hedgerow,
peeping through thorn
and rain, feathers sagging.
Huddled in the shadows, she waits
to break the dawn with hope.

## Saying Goodbye
### —after reading Anne Kennedy

It's always the stray beam
that catches the eye —
forget the shadows, the black
worries of night; step into that light.
Feel it surround, engulf you.
Look at it closely,
let it guide and keep you safe
because the darkness isn't that far away.

# I.

*the choir of evening descends*

## The Space Between Us

I am traveling from one September to another —
the surf's growl echoing a half-life.
Summer sighs good-bye to the bee,
to the slow days parroting each other
in blue perfection. Foolish
to mourn the equinox, leaves scratching the sky,

lobes spinning into brown crumbs as they must.

Gone the iris, the hollyhock, stalks shriveled
into dry needles. Hollows hug their shadows longer,
ridges baring themselves to the horizon,
stark until twilight blurs the seam.
It's always September now — gannets harping the wind,
promise of winter in its chill.

## Unlock the Door

In another time
in the dusk of your dream —

somewhere a bow strokes its violin,
frost shirring branches and windows,
    glittering under the moon,
an owl beckoning the night.

We don't live in that place,
                            in that peace
though we're always searching —

A parade of coffins tracks our minds,
stacks as massive as the pyramids,
sands spitting in a wailing wind.
                    Grit rips as deep
as grief, gets trapped on the empty plains —

an echo that bursts through your sleep:
                            we are here.

## The Lost Heart

Branches twist in February's wind,
rain usurped by snow,
dew turning into crystalled coins.
Cardinals color the feeder,
pulse in the gloom — their chirrups
echoing the yard and sage grass
as sun sets. Each tree branch frosted,
the choir of evening descends
into silence. Ice like braille lines
the entrance, cobwebs of moonlight
sifting spirits still tucked in crevices.
Maybe our loss is the miracle.
A shaman somewhere etches names
in the cave of the dead.

## All the Way Through

Queen Anne's Lace crochets the woods
while you unlearn love
knots and whipstitches,
hands harboring an ache
that doesn't disappear
no matter how warm.

This morning's breeze chased clouds
until the sun hovered overhead, a fist
hammering heat across the yard.
An ice-fire creeps up your spine, thrill
of a lover's touch
replaced by dread —
a struggle to let the air caress
as it scoops the space
your breasts used to fill.

The bright wine-patch of the hummingbird
bewitches you: fire and fermentation —
two things pumping now through your veins.
Heart the hero and the villain:
your body the victim.

# Grief

The doe stares until I turn away —
when I look back, she is gone.
No sound to tell me where,
no movement of the leaves.
Only the wind — breathing.

You left like that.
No gasping, no torturous sobs,
just a closing of your eyes,
and I was alone again.

Now I wander the woods,
hike trails where families laugh.
Where couples with dogs
smile and whistle,
where music pulses with runners,
invades the stillness of this place,
where once we towed
our own kids and dogs.

The dream, the reverie
that comes from silence, I need.
When summer sun sears
through canopies of green,
when heat hazes the path —
a shimmer — where I can see
a hind leg, a hoof — you—
appear in the shadows.

## Crowding Out the Light

Rain again, but roses still bud
blood-red against another gray day.
Clover beckons, white-tongued petals
licking the air even as bees hum,
nuzzle into kiss-colored centers.

Two years ago drought browned
the mountains, burned patches on ridges
where pine once shaded laurel and fern.
The woods smoked for weeks —
a reminder of the searing sun, if we needed one.

The finch fashioned her nest by the front door again.
Every year she scolds us for leaving,
for returning, her small shelter tucked behind
a wreath of lavender. When she startles
from her eggs, I apologize, an urge
to stop, to peer into that woven darkness.

I want to sink into what's left
of that protective warmth. To remind myself
the smallest hearts can beat in fear.

## Spring Tide

—for Rachel Held Evans

The sting of salt, of stones along the shore keeps me
    focused on the here, the now.
Mist slipping in shrouds the horizon,
        everything erased, including my thoughts.

    What was promised this morning,
the sun's sigil for the new day, the new month,
        has come to this: emptiness
so thick it presses my body, and I can't breathe,
        try to push it away but grasp . . . nothing.

    I want to creep into a closet, a dumbwaiter —
    hide in the smallest space to bear the weight
of this loss. Instead it saturates this wide place.
    I shout your name but only the waves and gulls cry back.

We are all searching for what's left (of you).
    But the wind snatches every atom, every fragment,
flings them out into the blue, the gray,
    the water, the spray as they pull away
        farther, farther until the empty strand stretches —

    ripples left in the sand
        where your footprints
        used to be.

# Cobwebs, Breathing

*I am glad it cannot happen twice, the fever of first love. For it
is a fever, and a burden, too, whatever the poets may say.*

—Daphne du Maurier

After the first flush of love comes the sickness
then the dying.
Trinkets of tickets, a teddy bear,
even a nubby flannel shirt
must be packed into a box
that becomes a coffin —
buried in the far corner of your closet.
Sometimes you even forget it's there.

No box will lock your thoughts, keep them
from bursting loose, so you blush
when a friend waves a hand
in front of you, asks what's wrong
then hesitates.          They know.
You were in a long ago place —
a place where rose petals were tucked away,
scent still staining your hands.

# Slow, Brief Watch

We thought spring had come early,
but crocus and robin roused false hope.

Now dusk brushes the city,
shadows the violet of nightshade

as snow confettis the grass, the streets
until white silence settles.

After the confusion of this week, a surprise
of softness,
like the kitten we discovered

in the back of the truck, mother gone,
twin already cold. Her mewl so thin

we almost missed it. We washed, fed her
milk with an eye dropper.
She loved
to curl near my neck, on your chest.

But the chambers of her lungs
were like cotton fluff. Not enough breath

for one short life.

Stillness deepens, more comfort than we thought,
as night winds closer, a lavender mantle

where streetlights and headlamps echo
                              the mounding snow.

## Mystery of Salt

The ocean breathes a ragged sigh,
    clouds sagging with rain.
Waking on a gray day takes concentration,
    an effort of will when a pool of warmth cradles
us close, covers snugged to our chins.
      Wind whistles the corner of the house,
mimics gulls crying, and I wonder
    if the storm will pass. If the briny air
will fill our eyes with tears.

Yesterday, sea and sky echoed
    a perfect blue, water smooth
enough to roll marbles as we stood
    in the prow, each of us taking turns
to hold you one last time.
      Even though we knew you were not there —
at least not in that coffer, that box —
    we included you in our conversation.
And before we let the ocean take you,
    heavier than we thought,
we kissed you like we could fill your lungs
    again.

To leave you in the dark, the deep
    was what you wanted. And with shore
so far away, we watched the spot
    where we left a bit of earth and ash,
with flowers scattered around,
    lone tern circling above.

This morning you are truly gone,
    and we face the coming storms without you.

## Living With Ghosts

Regret is a divided junkyard,
which is to say the piled clutter
by the fence line, the one that keeps people
out, and the regrets heaped in the middle
may as well be in different lots.
The rusted, broken pieces around the edge
have been scattered and scoped
by crooks and critters, sometimes
even friends. If asked, I tell them
they're welcome to them —
take as many as they can bear.
They usually only take one
or two. But the heart of the yard throbs
with emptiness — there's not even a hole,
just bare, raked dirt. Nothing comes
from not taking chances — the only regret
nobody wants, the only one
                          I can't throw away.

## Broken Moon

Lightning zippers the sky,
thunder cracking, roaring,
and the trail disappears
under seething rain.
Who knew the groundhog
would get it right?
Double red flags at the shore flap
and curl like crests along the beach,
palms bending into the wind.
Headlights like tiny diamonds
spark the gloom,
torrents gurgling across sidewalks and streets.
Easier to face this, forget my longing.
Let the wind rage, let me linger
at the edge, in the center
where no one can hear me.
If they ever did.

## No Way Back to What Was

Clouds stagger in March wind,
crocuses spearing the field.
I tried to save rain in the bowl
of my hands, but there's always a flaw,
a fissure that lets things go,
leaving me empty. I want
to offer a coin, an apple, the moon —
but nothing is right.

When the rhododendrons bloom,
when the bees drink from silken thimble-cups,
I will ask Saint Brigid
how she unfolded a field,
how she escaped forever into the hills
where hooded crows echo the skies.

How do I stay where the river birch bends
over empty creek beds?
Where tanks crush a car and driver
like we used to stomp beetles?
Where libraries and hospitals burn, ashes like snow?
March thunders into a future already cracking
like shells smashed onto shingled shores
clinging to sand, tide tugging,
dragging back to the deep.

## Darker Than the Ruined Sky
—Election Year 2024

Days of leaf-snap and blaze
finished, now branch and bark
gorge on rain, on sun beginning
to singe the horizon again.
Wren and barn owl, dogwood and holly:
a host of in-betweens yet we keep silent –
underestimate the slug, the fungi,
molecules coalescing into mist
that clouds our vision. Shadows shorten
these long days and an echo
of anger, of fear bleeds through the news.
Dusk fires the night, a haunting
of autumn as wind rattles past, uncovers
a red-streaked sea of stars.
Where do we go from here?

## Sorrows Multiplied

—line from William Butler Yeats

November and it's 80 degrees.
The full blood moon was in total eclipse
this morning — long before warblers
roused the dawn.
What's happened
to all we can expect — except the unexpected?
Gas prices, electric prices — all the prices
are up, up, up but even nature keeps throwing
curve balls: earthquakes in Indonesia,
New South Wales flooding, Mauna Loa
growling in the Pacific, Kentucky wildfires.
All this in November.
Retrieving the bird feeder after dark
I surprised a racoon on my deck.
Only I was more astonished
than he was — he sauntered down the stairs
and scaled the oak while I back-peddled
into the house. And, oh, the deer — so many sets
came through the yard this summer
I finally stopped counting.
Finches and chickadees are storing thistle
in some secret place — I've had to fill it
three times each week since August.
I don't know
if blizzard or famine is in our future, but, clearly,
something big is coming.
            If Bethlehem's *rough beast*
*slouches* toward us — the revelation may not be
as we believed.

## Footprints in Ash

Even now the land is rewilding.
After the fires, wastelands

where towns and forests once bloomed,
clouds bloated with dust cough
across a heated sky.

Scorpions skitter into crevices
to winnow the ashes, the grains
of what remains.

Trees, doors, people — broken.
Hammers without handles,

pens without ink,
bone without marrow — (all) useless.
Harbingers of what is to come.

But what of life past? Beauty
from memory, serenity from routine.

Poisoned with politics, we grope
in darkness and in light, hesitating

at the edge. Our gusto transformed
to granite, blood emulsified to sludge:

we become statues, ravaged
later or sooner.
The (re)wilding has begun.

## II.

*Salt scours my heart, sharp sting of loss*

# Fill the Ocean with Grief
   —for Victor

Grit leads from beach to trailer park under palms,
your blond hair warm, the color of sand washed by tides.
Did your body betray you as early as that?
Each day you corralled your little sister
and tucked her in bed, finished homework
before your mom came home. Another late shift
so the cupboards had cartons and cans
for you to open before school.

Or were you still surfing strong, free from any future
fear until you grew — traveled from Florida
up north to see your father, summers blistering
and steamy, no salt breeze to soak your skin?
Or was it when you married your Disney wife?
Dogs replacing babies, tugging the two of you
from one adventure to another — is this where the shadow
bit your blood like a poisoned apple?

No hint when we had dinner, the Virginia coast
keeping our vacation in check — another body of water to float,
to drown in. But, sometime, somewhere, your flesh
betrayed you — betrayed us all. You shuffled into sickness,
sank deeper into the unknowing: tongue like a sand dune
shifting your words — the rhythm of your heart
still strong like gulls crying, circling the gusts.

How do I write about an unfinished life?
Tomorrow we'll take you back to the ocean.
The long wait in white rooms, the measured beeps
and lights will recede to a nightmare barely remembered.
Only — you will not be here when we wake.

## Borrowed From the Grave

Kabul has fallen. Leaves shiver
in the sudden change. Heat-haze
for weeks, grass withered and worn.

A shift in the air, a breeze rushes through.
But we're a continent and an ocean away.

Berry-bright, cloaked and smothered:
what happens to the gardens of women
as seasons change in Afghanistan?

Vultures flex in cedars after hounding
an eagle. Far away, spiraling like a sirocco,
the Condor Galaxy stretches into blue stars.

Peacocks plucked, jackals pounce
the gazelles, muzzles red-soaked.

A gate opens, hinges shrieking
as boots, boots, boots stomp —
jasmine choking, honeycomb stripped.

Summer blisters on, clouds ghosting
the horizon. A thousand voices
in a desert full of bone and tooth.

I'm sure there were heroes.
(Where are they now?)

Rain only rumor, nowhere to hide
in thorns. The sun lashes olives,
fig and pomegranate tasting of salt.

Parched tongues cleave to our mouths.
Smoke in the distance becomes an inferno in the yard,
the doorway — ash spreads fast.

And the desert yawns wide, wider —

                                    torn and empty.

## Without Asylum
### 1981

We laughed into the dark kitchen
coming home one night still licking salt
and butter from our fingers, debating possibilities
of Indiana Jones finding the Ark,
just Mom and me, Dad still working out of town.
Heading upstairs to bed, Mom pushed me backwards,
hand over my chest like we were in a car
                             about to crash.

I didn't know what she was doing, why
she wouldn't speak,
only knew something was wrong
as she backed us out the side door
   to the driveway, stumbled
to the neighbor's for his phone.

What I didn't see then was the front-jamb, splintered,
     door leaning into the stairwell.
Radio, records, television all gone, just empty spaces,
strangers' words smeared across the walls,
the music and voice of our family silenced —
like my trust in coming home, believing it
   safe.

How do you live with fear?
When violation contaminates your core,
infests your privacy, renders everything
     untouchable,
when invaders have cracked the heart of your home,
exchanging a husk for your heart?

# Fear

It's a lichen crawling
over the barks of ruined oaks and pine,
scattering across rocks like spilled
crickets — a barren desert-scape
where sand swallows the sky,
slopes shape-shifting the horizon;
it's the scalped remains
of an autumn yard, wind betraying
the last warmth before winter,
a woodpecker drumming hollow logs.
It is sludge spilling over garbage bins,
an alley hazed with smog, shards of vinegar
and beer bottles gleaming greenly,
rusted rails of the subway fence
whining in a lonely street.
Whether the drab walls of waiting rooms
or the scuffed turf of an empty field,
the dented Maverick in an adjacent lot
or scarred scales of a trout lured
from an algae-filmed lake:
it waits.

## Unleashed

White sky here, birds hidden
somewhere in the hedgerows.
Another hurricane advancing to the Gulf —
we wait, air thickening.

           Kabul, its citizens, our soldiers —
clouds of liquid rubies hovering above the city:
souls still
         rising.

Shards chiseled from statues mean nothing.
      Nothing whole remains,

here where the sun devours
remnants, even the roots,
             of hope.
Sand shifts, dunes forming and flattening.

Winds whipped to Category Four,
we need the levees to hold,
to keep our belongings, ourselves
              unchanged.

Cattails, reeds in the marshland bow.
Echoes humming the waves,
tears in eyes filled with dust
from a land seared, scarred.
                Afraid.

## More Than Grief

This spring the snarling sea thrashes and bucks,
not even pelicans skim the surf.
Shells clatter onto the shingled sand,
kelp and bladderwrack at tug-of-war with the tides.
Salt scours my heart, sharp sting of loss
like the rasping surge and cry of geese,
even when nights spin a silky sea-mist,
smash of wave on wave, my thoughts scatter like spray.

Who can hide in one still spot where no stillness lies?
Low tide exposing a shore that slows you,
drags you back to the here, the now.
Hunched in wind and cloud, this sound
of the sea, this world roaring at me — and my heart,
all tender parts torn, rages and seethes.

## Waiting for Locusts
New Year's Day 2011; Beebe and Ozark, Arkansas

Wind sculpts birch and redwood,
smears the sky white. A willow leans,
dips tresses in the frosted pond.
Above the ridgeline, man and dog trudge,
slicing the light as they climb.

The air throbs with silence, no bird song
devours the dawn. Coop's field aches
in a flood of decaying blackbirds.
Flies storm the shiny sea of feathers, flesh.
Across town, Dale's Diner windows
a bevy of beaks and wings fixed
in flight, small heaps of muscle and meat
on the pavement, in every street.

A hundred miles away drum fish fracture
the lake's surface, scales glazing the light
as they pile around rocks, along banks,
eyes glaring at the heavens in silence.
So much silence.

## Fortune Is a Beggar

Star-shine streaked by lightning,
Harvest Moon smolders with clouds,
September heat steaming the rain.

Oil seeps from pipes, from drills,
from earth — black blood swelling
like an unkindness of ravens

that slips across ditches, fallow fields,
down the muted peaks of Appalachia,
sinks into the valleys' ruts and creases.

A bucket abandoned in sandbox shadows,
rusty gate whining with morning wind,
barn door open, listening for the *shush*
of encroaching wings.

## When We Get There, I Will Have Nothing to Tell

May's promise shaved by rain and chill,
this unexpected bite another reminder
we are not in control.
407 days sequestered left us hovering
our doorways, hesitating between safe solitude
and living.

Drawings of masks graffiti store doors,
burden us with more decisions
than what to buy —
now it's a matter of cost.
We saunter the sidewalks but still turn away
from others passing by, dogs and children skittish.
We no longer smile or say hello —
our very breath tainting the air.

We squint in the light, expect the world
to be changed and instead find ourselves
altered.
Unlike Birds of Paradise, we have languished
without sun, without benefit of anything
except rootedness
which we have clutched — exercising
our right to silence, to darkness.
Wondering why there is no song.

## Love Costs Everything

I always told myself
  the river would be a blessing —
  in the golden light of autumn,
the stark grays of winter,
  and in spring's leaping waterfalls
  rivers spin their magic.
But I've spent these days with loss
  scrubbing the stars,
    and the water's music has abandoned me.
Mimosas' woolly blossoms
  brush across the rocks
    beside dandelion fluff that didn't work.
What do I wish on
  when the night bristles
    with darkness — the half-moon hiding,
even the crickets mute?
  What can I remember
        that won't leave me
drowning?

## Giving Stones

Purple finches sculpt the trees,
wings hinged as they balance the upper branches,
silhouette the sky. Sunrise tempts their song,
feathers blending in early shadows.

I wish the news would blur grace
into these high, light notes of morning
for the coming day.
    But a neighbor attacks
from behind, ambush instead of conversation.
Words second place to fists, bruised
egos worth more than broken ribs.

How have we come to this?

Cardinals bully their way to the feeder,
wrens, nuthatch dodging the flapping wings —
hopping aside, fluttering away then back again.
None daring to abandon the gift of food,
of mercy these cold and bitter days.

## After Surgery

A pair of swans preen, slide
   swiftly across the blue cool
of lake — soon they will taste
   the frost before it comes and rise
together finding a thermal draft
   that guides them to warmer climes.

The lamps on each bedside table beckon,
   downy softness sandwiched
between them where letters turn to words
   that take dreams to flight:
promise of light before the final dark.

Following the trail as sure as scent,
   the wolf with smoky fur and tender heart
nuzzles his mate. She licks his ear
   while they pause beneath an evergreen
leaning with the weight of snow.
   Branches bristle, spear the feathery mounds.

Toes seek solace in fuzzy comfort,
   left and right slippers waiting by the door.
Twelve hours constricted in stiff leather
   pressing concrete pleads a soothing escape
to stretch and wiggle.

Seahorses couple, anchor themselves
   in the reeds, the grass. Undulating
they wrap around each other
   and daily dance invisible currents —
nodding to blennies and gobies, to kelp
   clinging across the rock and sand.

I didn't know I was grateful,
   with my eyes and ears and lungs,

to watch the moon twin the sun: two flawed
   globes that balance night and day —
lead the seasons, reel against the dizziness
   that unbalances my new walk, my new life.

## Falling Light

October leaps across the lawn,
   gold never quite parting with night —
a honeyed haze that will soon vanish
   in a lavender dusk. Light-glow
through leaves on the marsh shift
   into long, low shadows. This patchwork
month of warm days, cold mornings, mist and sun.
   Leaving home wrapped in layers,
I return with them over my arm.
   The hummingbirds vanished overnight,
chickadees in a frenzy over thistle.
   Anticipating a winter of want,
they store the future in their bellies,
   stuff their nests like I stash chocolate.
I've pulled out the quilts, stored the patio chairs,
   and now I wait.
Wait for the unknown, the unknowing
   to fill me as sunset slips into a darkness
that crouches ever closer.

## Season of Salt

After the burn of summer
was the letting go,
sky unchained,
learning a different blue.
Fields pocked and clumped
spilled scorched breath
into the hollers,
around the hulk
of the mountains, far
into its crannies and clefts.
No tenderness left,
no autumn abundant
with the melody of leaves.
No creeks kissing,
tumbling grassy banks.
No. Lifting our eyes
to face the dark, we pause.
Only the ruins remain.

## The Unraveling

After the solstice our long slide
    into night begins. We barely notice.
Toes in surf and sand, we scour
    the everyday from our bodies —
spray streaking our skin,
    savoring salt on a lover's lips.
We won't see it until the first leaf
    falls, when bees caress fading daisies
with long slow sips instead of zipping
    from clover to stonecrop, bellies
and legs sloughing golden dust.
    The equinox will come and go
before we lift our eyes to tangled twilight
    and wonder how we got here —
how far there is to go.

# III.

*the bargain with light has begun*

## The Almost Invisible

There's mystery in gray skies —
   a sanctuary in the mist,
the softness of dove wings,
   the luminescence of sea pearls
beckoning from coral and sand.
   Between music and pain,
it's a shade that wanders
   in wind, cloud, and storm,
tastes like sleep and ink,
   dreams lost in fog
and hydrangeas' chalk-white petals.
   Gray slips like smoke
into the space between passion
   and heartbreak, pebbles
spilling from the tip of the tongue.

## Catching Moonlight

The devil's crescent moon rides high,
slices the tangle of stars while we wait,
each one in her own place, for a new dawn.

Darkness crouches close, blurred by bits
of fog — something at least we can see
coming closer then shrouding us,

eclipsing that gilt fingernail
that is barely light enough.

Doves and cardinals finish
their late night carols, disappear
into tufts of honeysuckle, forsythia —

one just budding, the other weeping
golden petals across the yard.

When the sun nudges night away,
we will rise and explore the ruins
           of what we used to know.

## Unsay the World

Pink moon sings
  the curfew of March,
robins dimpling the yard
  as I head to work. Grim, gray
city freezing, spring shrouded
  and haunting our thoughts.
Snow slush piled beside streets
  and signs create a wall
of ice, resistance snagging
  salt and rain: shrinking,
but not fast enough.

If we could transplant
  these slabs to the stars,
is space cold enough
  they would survive forever?
Or would starlight melt
  them so fast there's no time
to grow a rose?
  What if the moon howls
itself into oblivion?
  Constellations dim and die?
Would we still dream in a dark so dark?
  Dare even to close our eyes?

## Color of Blood and Shadow: Lament for Autumn

You're painting rain
   into this dazzling day.
Don't worry, your secret
   is safe with me, *cuisle mo chroidhe.*
I know your heart is locked
   in loss, no way to pivot
without spiraling into a white abyss.

But I long for your laugh
   between the cedars, the way
you pause before answering
   the woodpecker and twilight
with a frosty kiss. How, curious,
   you lick each dawn with mist
rising from valleys and lakes.

How you rain gold, red, and rust.
   How the taste of earth is just a short sleep
before beginning again.

Irish Gaelic: (cushlamochree): vein of my heart/sweetheart

## What Cannot Be Changed

Even with Samhain closing in,
   there's no fog or mist
that divides the living and the dead.
   I'm already a ghost —
a brief blur you might remember.
   No halo around the hunter's moon
where clouds hover then shrug
   and move on. Maples and oaks shuffle
what's left of their leathered leaves,
   bear the crow as he balances
between midnight and morning.

## The Burden of Memory

June's green quivers with desire,
sky wet with light and promise.
Purpletop shifts, whispers the field,
milkweed listening
to the barn creak and groan.

After winter's bitter bite,
swallows scuffle air
across scarred and spidered beams.
News littered with earthquakes,
spewing hate from race to race.

I come here to breathe,
watch clouds scatter the sky,
seize the apple before it falls.

## Between Moments

Sea mist erases the shore,
    dim shadows in growing gray.
  The sob of surf sounds
both hollow and close as water searches
    the rock, the sand —
  the bargain with light has begun.

The dog, more nimble than I,
    leads as I slip across a harvest of sea-wrack.
  Curlews cry and curse from within
the cottony fog so much like a womb.
    I wait, shrouded and blind,
  bell buoys clanging somewhere with the tide.

Kelso tongues salt off stone,
    nudges driftwood until a crab scythes the air
too near his nose. Folded in this flannelled haze,
  I laugh while he snuffles and skitters the sand,
    barks drifting into nothing.

Sunlight seeps through mist,
  seeds of water charming the air
in a fading dance as dunes, seagrass,
    docks sculpt the horizon —
  rumors of the world taking shape once more.

## The Darkness We Carry

Rain lashes the windows —
    lightning silent and bright in the midnight hours.

Each flash highlights fog whisking the drenched yard,
    and gusts shudder the house. The shush of rain

keeps me shifting from window to window
    as it drizzles then pours, fresh buds knuckling

under the weight of water. Pansies' purple shadows
    against copper leaves, bruises

in the snow, now bow in the squall —
    promise of dawn's rescue too far away.

This, at least, I can see.
    Unlike a handshake or a hug shedding germs

like a malicious godmother dusting rooms
    with seeds that choke us into wheezing sleep.

Tomorrow it will be so easy to scorn
    this blustery night once mauve rinses the early sky

and finches fill the air in a gleeful key.
    To forget the grief that opened our eyes,

that nailed the reminder in our hearts
    that *now* is all that is.

## Moments, Rightly Placed

At dusk
when anything
could crack open,
heat lightning
and katydids fill
twilight's shell.
The air hangs
thick and heavy,
and we gulp
the darkness
as it spills —
weight of the day's
words, worries
sifting away.
A breath
of stars stirs
the sweetgum, the poplar —
thin edges
of light
searing, burning
the remains
of the day.

## Variations on a Text

—line from Louise Glück

*There are infinite endings,*
so which do we choose?
The clock where time ticks down,
the wail of a winter storm,
the race up winding asphalt
where a deer surprises
our hands on the wheel —
a lurch then sailing the stars?

For every certain beginning
has its uncertain ends,
and the trail we hiked yesterday
might tomorrow be tangled in gloom,
and the wishes we whisper
into dandelion fluff may abandon
the seeds into sand or water or dirt.
Do we swallow the loneliness
or accept the chaos of crowds?

This season is almost over,
snow beginning to fall.
A waning crescent pulses,
we can feel it there,
wrapped in layers of clouds
while stars flicker and call.

## All We Are

Sometimes you have to let go
   of fear, release it like a balloon
      from your freeing fingers.
   What you have left isn't emptiness.
Turn your hand so the palm
   is toward the sky: a plea?
      An offering?
   What you breathe in is what you hold —
your very life.
   Each invisible molecule awakens
      to the energy of this earth:
   every worm tunneling the soil,
every crocus lifting petals in spring,
   daylilies nodding to the sun,
      the nightingale serenading each moon.
   Watch the balloon, embraced by blue,
consumed,
   until even its speck is gone.

## Listen for the Roots

Rain tiptoes through the leaves,
woods singing under a slur of fog.

Six days draped in gray,
and I can hear the trees breathe.

Beneath leaf-scatter, daffodils are stirring,
the only sign of sun.

A robin trills, squirrels skittering
around pines, claws scrabbling the rough bark.

It's been a long winter.

Westerly winds breach hibernation's heart,
arrow through the atoms of each cluster

of dirt and stone so that even the bedrock
blossoms in warmth.

## Design Restored

A choir of snow sings
   twilight's silence, feathered flakes
hushed as they caress then hug
     the cradles of trees, leaf heaps,
fields furrowed and splotched.

Monochrome of crow and rock
   outlined against the white sky:
my eye a bright coin,
     my breath twisting from vapor
into nothingness.

A world blank, ready to re-shape.

This time, let's use cobwebs
   and honeybee pollen
instead of concrete and drills —
     the only gouging
done by the woodpeckers' beak,
   the beavers' grooved teeth.

Let's start again
   with this blue-green bead polished
and pulsing on a sable cape
     nodding to the Pleiades,
sipping from the Dipper —
   a harmony, a rhapsody
like angels humming
     something almost remembered.

## Becoming a Horizon

A calling from the trees, a sudden sound
   swelling from branch to branch,
surrounding me.
The air fills, quivers with a gulp
   of swallows then I see it —
a falcon coaxed by thermal tides,
golden wings stretching in the light
   that lingers. Like a growl rumbling
from the neighbor's cat over its nest
of bones, the air vibrates until it moves on.

Back home I run a bath, waver
between salts or bubbles — bits of mineral
   for my aches or silky feathering for a treat?
Room warm and steaming, my skin pinks.
Perched on tub's edge, my foot hovers,
   tests the heat. Water welcoming, I slide in,
dream hollow bones, heavy flesh, a chance to sing.

## Light Dissolving

A fist of wind curves the branches where crows laugh
in a fringe of beeches. Twilight detaches from the sagging sun,
silhouettes braiding the yard. Across the neighborhood,
a plainsong of light vibrates through windows,
but I prefer to sit in darkness, think of my uncle losing his sight,
following his mother's lead. What becomes of us
in the dark that is ours alone? When only shadows severing
our light tells us something has changed? The stir of air
that wasn't there before. Will I sour in silence, in blindness?
Will I think of maples blazing the autumn woods
    and seafoam on sand,
a fox darting across the backyard, bluebirds ruffling
    in the birdbath?
Or will I open myself to sound and taste and touch
    that are still mine —
children giggling next door, honey swirled into tea, your lips
whispering my cheek, guiding me home.

## Every Grief You Have Not Said

Breathing the ashes of dreams,
I slip to the strand, waves beckoning.
The curve of moon flickers like a gaslight
between clouds, rain promising.
Sand shifts, scours my feet as I climb
the dunes, sea oats and saw palms dim silhouettes.
Metronome of surge and suck remind me
the ocean throbs with secrets, unshareable.
Striding the tideline, salt spray beads
my skin, echoes of ghosts hissing in foam.

And you — where are you now?
Scattered like the shells,
like silverfish that whirl the depths?
When we let you go, did you return?
Or did you drift to other shores,
a cove, a key maybe — a place, finally, to rest?

## Last Hour of the Tide

Gulls and cormorants scrape a paper sky,
   shriek above seas marbled with veins of foam
that chide and hiss the shoreline. A bell buoy clanks
   in slinking mist — distance disappearing.
Plovers peep along the rim of sand and sea.
   Rain later today, but we expect that — know that just beyond
what we can see is another storm. We wait —
   watch the haze bloom lighter, brighter
before a surge of gray spools through, thunder offshore.
   A gust brushes ghostly fingers across the strand.
Closer. Then rain pummels what's left
   of blue haw, sea oats, smacks the dunes, the boardwalk.
Nature still in control here, at the edges of a continent
                                changing.

## Leaving Song

Even the leaves slip into similar shades
of thick-skinned pumpkins lining the porches, the steps.

Gusts burst from the north, apple trees bare-fisting,
their fruit decaying in gold and brown decadence.

What happened to honeysuckle vining
the oaks, trumpeting summer's glory?

Nothing protects them now,
blackberries and lavender withered to knobs.

The silver promise of moonlight's sonata
sings through the shroud enclosing us,
veiling the remains of hope.

Soon the Hunter's Moon will lead the winged
horse across a darkening sky, arrows of light
pointing the way through this long, now longer night.

Watch how the leaves, when they let go,
dance with the wind.

## What Wind Knows

Wind blusters the canopy of trees,
   clouds bruising a marbled sky.
Chimes whirl and sing
   while the chickadees hide.
Yesterday's sun burnished a falcon
   gliding through the blue
golden feathers stretched wide.
   I couldn't look away —
wildness at large.

Today a different kind of wildness:
   fury of leaves spattered with rain,
gusts mistaken for thunder,
   rush of wind against my face.
These days,
        each day,
a measure of grace,
   a reminder I am
not in control,
   not of where the light falls,
not of the dropping blossoms
   that look like snow. Breathe
in this moment —
        now let it go.

## At Last the Rains Came

The tin roof talks
in the rain, shames
the drip and drizzle
echoing onto the lake.
Boats moored
at the docks knock,
duckweed squashed.
Sweltering
before the storm,
a bridge buckles
in soaring heat.
But now cool air sways
under bruised clouds.
Through windows, lightning
chisels the lake's surface,
electricity humming.
In a porch corner
an orb-weaver, home
scorched then swamped,
waits, eager to create
a newer, better place.

# IV.

*night's elegy on their tongues*

## Always Fall Forward

And one day the trees grew green again,
shadows shaved by a brighter sun.
Breath bottled by winter's chill burst into song,
and eyes half-closed overflowed
with crickets and crows calling in the hedgerows.
A red-bellied woodpecker drums his love
on a poplar, iris quivering at attention,
waiting for the other feather to fall.

Oh, how snowfall convinced us,
fooled us with clean blankets,
nothing to show. But when ice melted
to water warmed to dew, quiet violets
ignited the memory of you
and me. And when light scribbled the horizon,
we measured the distance —
found how close (how very close) we'd come.

## A Measure of Hope

The ragged edge of summer tangles
limbs and branches as wind scours
   leaves already yellowed, confused
by damp and fog, stealing starlight
before the equinox. Hunter's Moon
   hides behind a pearl-pale sky.
Nuthatches whistle from the hedges,
pin the cat's ears and twitches her tail,
   considers. August's dust now dewed,
puddling beneath browning hydrangeas.
Mint and lavender, parched,
   litter the ground. Rain puzzles the scars
of summer — each cracked vein
filling, cleansing, healing.

## Fire Has No Memory

What I missed was an anchor,
   the one friend who understood
each loss — until that loss was you.
   It's silly to talk of broken hearts,
burned bridges when each day
   is another ladder-rung to struggle,
each morning starting again at the bottom.
   Each sleepless night clinging to a step
that cracked under the rough weight
   of emptiness. What you missed
was me gathering the pieces,
   heaping the ashes and emerging
like a phoenix — blazing, rising, wild.

# Dance the Crumbling Floor
### —after Damian Gorman

*If I was us, I wouldn't start from here* —
  past the first kiss, the blush, the flush
that flamed our bodies . . .
  when looking into your eyes there was time enough —
time expanding minutes and hours
  into memories that forever shape us,
our connections with others.

*If I was us, I wouldn't start from here* —
  with three a.m. trips to the bathroom
and aches in joints that used to bend smoothly
  as we jogged or boxed, after the cramps in fingers and toes
made handshakes and hiking more painful
  than we thought when our grandparents said the same.

Who would know the gray hair, the white hair,
  the no hair wouldn't matter; that laugh lines and wrinkles
only enhanced the spirit beneath our fading glory?
  Already weary and set in our ways but recognizing
who we are: choosing more carefully, more wisely
  like a full-bellied cat tempted with an unsought treat.

But maybe I would, would start from here:
  recognizing that stillness can be healing,
that the discerning house finch turns her head
  only at the unusual, the unexpected.

Mavbe I'm glad,
  I'm glad we didn't start
                    from there.

# Answer the Moon

Remember the ocean, each molecule
of water, each grain of salt, how it rises
and falls, lifts and tugs you under,
singing her song along each wave and swell.

Remember the wind, each season drifting in
at just the right time: summer sun to dry
sodden spring, a kaleidoscope of leaves
before winter's branches scratch the sky.

Remember fire, how the flames dance for joy
or anger — how they burn or refine, licking
air and wood, flesh and bone:
crucibles sculpted with lightning.

Remember the earth, how soil feels in your hands:
fistsful that fill your heart, calm your thoughts
and hum with you as you lean close, closer.

Remember.

## Unfiltered After Fifty

Fear seized, trapped me once too often.
I let it fester, scar an ugly green
like the pencil lead a boy jammed in my thigh
in seventh grade when I wanted to open my mouth,
sing about moonstone and malachite,
ghost of the writer already breathing in me.
But my tongue furred,
jaw clamped then rusted shut.
I wished I lived when monks inked
parchment and vellum, quills scratching
and tapping in forgivable silence.

The woodpecker now my totem:
   unrepentant in her brash staccato, commanding
her space, boundaries extended
   as she needs — her perforation of trees
unmistakable,
        a wild castanet,
                    Unquenchable.

## Every Scar Has an Edge

Wind-bruised oaks welcome warbler-kissed dawn,
last night's Wolf Moon covered with clouds and flurries.
Mounds shroud the bushes, the house,
yard an unbroken desert of white.

My uncle called, haunted by his long-dead wife,
daughter becoming her eternal roommate.
The two of them whispering in his ear,
inflaming dreams, dreams.

But here are the bluebirds, the lark,
night's elegy on their tongues.
Not every goodbye offers closure.

River birch sluffs its bark as snow dissolves
its damp path to the ground —
and it comes back to this:

a squirrel leaping for a limb,
starlings gleaming near the feeder,
a candle still burning after last night's storm.

## Aim at the Wilderness

I follow where she leads,
  her nose relishing the unknown.
The wilds of our walk call to her.
    Where I see the same houses, the same
trees, she pays no attention.
  A squirrel in our yard would have sparked leaps
around trees, frantic barking.
    But here one rushes two feet past,
and her nose wriggles and snuffles
  along a path only she knows.
She stops, pushes her snout a little closer,
    a little further into the grass, the dirt,
tail wagging, hind paws dancing.
  To be that eager, that excited
about anything — to shut out all
    but this moment, right now.
The holiness of that — ahh, the secret.

## The Sigh
—after Ted Kooser

You look out the window and sigh,
and the trees shake their locks
whispering the secret of comfort –
to bend with the burden of wind,
to let a river of rain fall when it must,
to scorch in heat and from ice
yet sing each season, reaching
into a wide blue promise,
knowing you are not alone.

## Becoming

In the beginning she was tired.
   But she didn't have to be.
All choices were hers —
   are hers. And she can begin
in another direction any time.
   Look at her life-map,
the way she spends her time.
   Is it the business of life
that makes her tired or
   her busy-ness in it? Watch
as she decides where
   to place her foot next.
She wavers. Safety
   is in the sameness, but
safety hasn't been her friend
   in a long time. She takes a step.

# Heart, Full of Seed

Wind thrashes the oaks, scatters acorns
against the metal roof where squirrels will feast.
This room, warm and snug, embraces me.
Though the sun has risen and blues the sky,
frost veils the cars, the yard, my heart.
So many years I shaped you as the villain,
but I want to let that go.

A splinter moon sets my mind wandering.
Do you remember finding me on that midnight trail
when the rescue searchers couldn't?
How you even brought a thermos of hot tea
and pulled socks from your pocket? You were the light
I knew would shine. And you shattered me.

But the shards I have gathered are trimmed in gold —
the edges of every scar shimmering with wisdom,
even a kind of peace. Blow, wind. Go ahead
and toss the branches. Blow. Drop the loose,
the weak, the rotten things and watch me
turn them into gifts.

## Words, By Heart

I want to believe
Elizabeth Barrett's last whisper
to her husband's *How do you feel?*

How do we live? How shall we die?
No simple answers.

Each person stitches
the threads of his own life,
watches death loom only over her.

Will we be singing
as we stay or go?

Will we face forward
or keep looking back?

Her answer:

      *Beautiful.*

## Blessing of the Birds

Day begins in mist — white and gray
   linen haunting the dawn.
I take tea to the porch, wait
   for cardinals to kiss
with beaks full of seed,
   for bluebirds to puff and ruffle feathers.

Steam from my cup a scrim
   for hummingbirds buzzing like motorboats.
It's been a grueling week,
   and the woodpecker hammers suet, hickory
like I've wanted to pound my fist.

Let the too-plain throat of the wren trill
   her silky notes until the haze burns blue,
cup empty — melodies and harmonies harvested,
     lifting,    lifting.

## The Root of the Wind Is Water

Wind shreds the clouds,
   tears them across the horizon.
Gone the peachy glow of dawn,
   and now waves crest and foam,
roar their trouble to the shore,
   salt crusting the seaweed
tangled on shingle. Fleeting glimpse
   of a gull's carcass dragging the sand
before the tide tugs her out once more.
   Ridges of rock appear and disappear
in seaspray.

             Days like this,
   no others on the strand,
I remember how small I am,
   how unlikely to matter to this wildness
raging before me. Here I learn
   to be alone, to know the world will keep
going without me. But my bone
   and muscle grasp, grip the ledge
where I stand — doused by spume,
   uncaring of time, a mess of kelp wrapped
around my feet. *I belong, I belong —*
   my shouts carry to the sea.

## The Polish of Rain
—for Austen and Aisling

Sidewalk slicked with rain,
yesterday's chalk rinsed away —
the heart, the flowers, the naming.
Each meticulous line they shaped
on the driveway — gone, like so much magic.
The sort that doesn't long let
you keep the smiles, the songs.

Two swallows have staked their claim
under the porch eaves, and each time
I open the door, they startle
into the closest trees. They would have me
use another means to leave my house.
So would I — these days of inside
looking out grow thin. What can I say?

Blue blusters through the clouds,
tumbles them out of the way,
and a weak spring sun peeks through.
The girls come back, consider the blank canvas
of concrete and begin again.

I wish it were that easy —
to erase what was broken, what has passed.
Take joy as it comes, where I can.

## Portions

Morning half gone when light
   glosses the leaves like spun glass
and clouds heather the sky,
   cardinal voices sparking the trees.
Construction chinks and clangs down the street,
   plagues my head, and I teeter
between nature and — not.
   Cicadas vibrate the air, tires hum the road.
I drink tea, hear
   Arkansas and Louisiana drowning
while we ache for rain.
   A balance between too much
and not enough.

Air conditioners wheeze to life —
   a deer startles from the yard's edge.
I heap the feeders then flap away squirrels,
   and a cat haunts chipmunks through vinca.
A pileated woodpecker and a hummingbird brunch
   together. How many times do I miss this —
absorbed in the un-breathing shadows
   of my mind? Today I will smile
at the towhee surprising goldfinches
   and bluebirds scuffling for a spot,
the sun painting the woods a palette of greens,
   a peace lily unfurling its bud.

# V.

*stardust breathing*

# Peace Lies Curled

The cherry trees intruded
my gloom today. A week of rain
and last night's quick frost
left me stooped and crouched
in clouds of gray.

But this morning's air stunned us,
a chilly nip with the rising,
rioting sun. Bluebirds hush
as we listen to pink buds
humming into flower.

## In a Dry Month

Late afternoons the sky mopes —
dark clouds, heat lightning but no rain.
A promise that comes to nothing.
Then a kind of blue takes over, shards
of sun stubbling shadows across ridges, valleys.
The acoustics of thunder roll
between mountains, drowning the cicadas'
steady whine. Each year we hear
their rasp, their hum, notes fading, souring
as summer wanes like the lavender and thyme,
the resin on pine. Don't cry. Autumn storms
will soon come, trees shouting with color.

## Leafspear of Light

From a graveyard of pines
a towhee trills, one voice box gliding
into the second, an answer farther in the woods.

I might imagine them dreaming
as silhouettes of dogwood branches lace
the forest floor, what's left of last winter's storms.

Clouds pebble the sky, almost glued
to an excruciating blue. March grumbled in,
now a brilliance of forsythia and redbud.

Today we too can sing out of our losses,
take the shadows for what they are —
ephemeral darkness — no weight, no substance.
                              Only stardust.

## Rain, Whispering

The tension of summer surrenders,
ruptures as rain trickles in from the sea.
Commas of crows loiter in branches suddenly bare
though hummingbirds dashed south last week.
How do they know sanctuary is over?
That they can no longer squander
nectar in futile bursts of rivalry? This drizzle,
these low clouds foretell the measured freeze
that already begins to shadow us. Daylight shaved
into finer slices as we trip our way toward the solstice,
toward the silence that flows then settles
around us like the sifting snow. The steam of our breath
rising in air bittered by ice, rising like the sound of stars —
feathers brushing the coming dark.

## How the Light Gets In

Just past the surface,    water wrinkles
    in a riptide, pulls and tugs,    pushes
its way past reef and rock    as salt and sand
    whirl in the waves,    foam bright in the air.

Limestone fissures,    gray furrows
    that change,    split with the rain,
droplets    that seep and settle,
    lick the stones' roughness    until it surrenders.

Boulders spill    down the mountainside,
    thunder through a canopy    of trees and oh
how the forest    flourishes — performs a magic
    on the sleeping seeds    in moss and leaf rot.

The pieces    of whatever's left
    inside my chest    begin to soften,
edges    smoothed by time —
    shadows        shrinking…

## Yorkshire Wolds
—Poetry Bench at Huggate, Yorkshire, England

Resting on this bench
in the background I hear cars
then crows and, finally, the wind.
No matter the mizzle, the mist.
Now the muse is upon me,
carries my dreams through this dale,
winding, braiding the hawthorn
as they escape into the wolds –
loud with the echo of my words.

## Fragments of Grace

Autumn winds release leaves,
   the ache of loss orbiting
     the yards and woods. We savor
   the sun, its losing. Pray
for its pale light to wrap
   around us — days like glass, sharp
     and clear, not too far away.

   Mornings misty as wraiths,
noon still finds our breath
   frosting the air where crows crowd.
     So many, their cries a calliope,
   all the keys hammered at once.

Tattered leaves, stems and cupules
   peeled from acorns crumble
     into the earth — welcoming
   what nurtures the seeds waiting
for snow and ice to pass
   before lifting hopeful heads.

# When They Sing

Blades burst through the soil,
dusk tumbling into an oasis
of pastels, fog daubing the sky.
A steady breeze starches daffodils
glowing in the gloom. This long winter,
snow dusting every cleft and surface,
curved darkness to more darkness
until I was more fragile than the ice.
Even the cardinals found somewhere else
to nest their cheery notes, that flash of red
through empty trees nowhere to be found.

But now —
now the bluebirds are back, chickadees
hopping past wrens, each greeting the others,
making way at the feeder.
Each in its turn taking, sharing, fussing, waiting.
This night not so bleak, Worm Moon wriggling
into the sky — bits of forsythia
and dogwood peeking around the yard.
Winter is almost over,
even its black and white memory fading
to gray, serenading a new season,
   a new song.

# Through Fog, Through Storm, Stars

The spare days are gone —
redbuds and dogwoods bursting
along the ridges, rash colors splashing
the woods while we wait,
parched and paralyzed by something unseen.
Should we offer coins? Flowers?
It seems only blood will do.
No use denying this Janus-faced spring:

blossom-light veiling fear and loneliness.

Time has slowed and widened,
smoke of our winter fires dissolved
by the sparrows', the robins' songs.
A chain of notes that will lift us
past the lip of summer
where new moons will greet the night.
Something to wish on, to reach for —
darkness felled by the stardust breathing in us.

## Anti-Lament

For all the *nos* you were told,
say *yes*.
Yes to the opportunities that came anyway.
In spite of.
When you missed the last days of your grandfather,
hearing too late of the stroke, the coma,
but you remember his large, calloused palm
around your hand at the flea market, snuggling
into his side at American Legion meetings.
For the no to having a brother or sister, for the no
to having your own children,
you are thankful for the many rooms-full
of students you have cried and laughed with,
witnessed that ember of understanding.
Those who will keep in touch, who give you a hug
when they see you at the grocery store or at the mall.
For the no to the job in London,
remember the yes to seeing other countries,
putting your feet in foreign seas.
For the no to the marriage that didn't thrive,
for the no to a body without scars,
for all the wisdom you learned
the hard way, there was another way
that became yours. That became you.
A yes to love again.
For the no to living by the ocean
there was a yes to four seasons.
To mountains that move with the mist,
to fields waving with coreopsis and coneflowers
and leaves the colors of sunset.
A yes for when you wake in the morning
surrounded by darkness,
dawn blossoming just beyond your walls.

## To a Red Bird,

the only light as dusk spills
through larch and tamarack, slips
over sweetgrass.
You serenade the waning moon,
warm my thoughts, hands outstretched,
in winter's frost.
Bears dream about that bright breast,
cage of your breath flittering through hazy
twilight answering fireflies.
Heartwood of the forest, you are hope
singing as darkness descends.

## Weight of the Soul
### —with thanks to Emily Dickinson

Night kisses the cardinal's song
with the luster of dusk, embraces the edge
of all I can see. The way you linger
and fill every atom of empty space.
The chestnut-oak's gold but already veined
and outlined in brown, mauve mums fading
into white, and, oh, the boughs
that keep baring their limbs!
I know the grieving speak
a different language, but I hope you understand —
the bluebirds are still here — just —
and they flit from feeder to porch,
watch wrens lost in the open garage.
I know the ruin is within. But Spring,
  Spring will come again.

## Equinox

Veins of Lenten roses echo dragonfly wings,
daffodils patches of sunlight — a promise
of Spring, though tomorrow both may bow
their heads to ice or showers.
Steel drums and maracas surge
from a passing car, splash the air,
and I can almost taste the sea.
      But not yet.
Roots grip the warming soil,
leaf and petal breathing wind.
Today I lean toward the sun, light lapping
my skin, shadows sinking behind.

# Mending

Redbuds purpling the ridge confess
the damp, the dew that murmurs
during night's oblivion, no longer ransom
to the parchment of leaves crackling
the woods, the edges of shadows.
*Breathe*, mourning sighs.

Listen to rain braiding the branches
as they stretch toward a warmer light,
sap sealed in roots seeking remembered heights —
the river laughing to the falls,
cartwheeling beyond its snow-capped birth.
We confuse these wonders with chaos.

But it's no mistake
when robins scout worms,
squirrels chuckle the sweetgums,
and forsythia blazes a sky cracked
with our fear —
the rumor of winter has passed,
collect the embers.
Taste wonder again.

## How Is It, the Light

Even the leaves sing here —
   sprinkled with gold, russet, ruby.
A belt of spruce scrapes the blue,
   tips twitching a harmony
to elm, beech, black gum.
   Mornings licking blueberry syrup,
buttered rum evenings
in Maine, cranberries kissing our lips.
   Signs propped in shop doors:
      SEE YOU NEXT YEAR!
The force of winter waits
   like a vast dragon ready to pounce,
blistering with tongues of ice.
   Gold flawed in the waiting.
For now we'll collect the sun
   as it grazes the shore,
bear witness to ebbing green,
   hope lingering in our hands.

## Something Given

Bees surge through zinnias,
silver skippers drifting past.

August haze heats the streets,
asphalt after storm — steaming.

We wait for the light, we wait
for the wind: all we ever do.

Collect the nectar, the pollen now —
when will we pass this way again?

Ravens linger in the branches, note our heart-
beats while we consider the dark

clouds on the horizon, a flawless
blue over our heads. Always.

And when we come to the end,
as we will, the song and the silence

will have been enough.

KB Ballentine lives and works in southern Appalachia and earned her MFA in Creative Writing at Lesley University in Cambridge, Massachusetts. When not shuffling letters into words into lines, she enjoys hiking, reading, and traveling. Her books are published with Blue Light Press, Iris Press, Middle Creek Publishing, and Celtic Cat Publishing, and her work also appears in anthologies including *Women Speak* volumes 9, 8, and 7 (2024, 2023, 2022), *I Thought I Heard a Cardinal Sing* (2022), and *The Strategic Poet* (2021). Learn more at www.kbballentine.com.

Sheila-Na-Gig Editions

Because of this, during the Millennium, Earth will not be entirely perfect, for many will not turn away from their sinful nature. However, they will cause no serious problems, as Jesus will not allow significant issues to arise. God's moral laws will not be broken, and any problems will be immediately addressed. This discipline will not be mean-spirited but rather firm, just, and fair. Who could stand against the Son of God?

"For to us a Child is born, to us a Son is given, and the government will be on His shoulders. And He will be called Wonderful Counselor, Mighty God, Everlasting Father, Prince of Peace. Of the increase of His government and peace there will be no end. He will reign on David's throne and over his kingdom, establishing and upholding it with justice and righteousness from that time on and forever. The zeal of the Lord Almighty will accomplish this." — *Isaiah 9:6–7 (NIV)*

After the thousand years, Satan will be released. Those who refused to accept Jesus during the Millennium will follow Satan in an attack against Israel. This group will include people from all nations.

"On that day, when all the nations of the earth are gathered against her, I will make Jerusalem an immovable rock for all the nations. All who try to move it will injure themselves." — *Zechariah 12:3 (NIV)*

At this moment, Satan and all his followers—both human and demonic—will be thrown into the lake of fire and will be destroyed. Sin will no longer exist and will never again be known.

"Do not be afraid of those who kill the body but cannot kill the soul. Rather, be afraid of the One who can destroy both soul and body in hell." — *Matthew 10:28 (NIV)*

"A little while, and the wicked will be no more; though you look for them, they will not be found." — *Psalm 37:10 (NIV)*

What kind of personal relationships can the redeemed expect during the Millennium? In my mind's eye, I see myself contemplating a task assigned by the Lord Jesus to my soulmate and me. When I mention this to my soulmate, she quickly responds and provides a very good way to accomplish the task. Pretending I hadn't asked her, I appear as though I'm deeply in thought. After a few moments pass, I say, "I know!" Then I repeat word-for-word exactly what she had just suggested, concluding with, "Wow, that was a brilliant idea I just came up with—I don't know why I didn't think of it sooner."

The look I receive from my soulmate is priceless. She rolls her heavenly eyes and slowly shakes her beautiful head. As she does this, I see the realization dawn upon her that this playful exchange is something she'll continue to experience throughout eternity. Nearby, I observe Jesus standing quietly, smiling warmly. For the One who created humor knows that humor rooted in love is indeed a good and joyful thing.

The thousand-year Millennium and how it will unfold is viewed differently by Christian scholars. The three major positions on this subject are Postmillennialism, Premillennialism, and Amillennialism.

www.ingramcontent.com/pod-product-compliance
Lightning Source LLC
Chambersburg PA
CBHW071202120626
46546CB00006B/2382